HUGE AND HUNGRY

Contents

Simon Cheshire

Story illustrated by
Martin Chatterton

Heinemann

In this story

 Ben

 Ruby

 Mum

 Dad

Tricky words

- time machine
- brilliant
- dial
- suddenly
- roared
- listening
- vanished

Introduce these tricky words and help the reader when they come across them later!

Story starter

Ben lives with his mum and dad and his sister, Ruby. Ben loves to invent new machines. One day, he invented a time machine that could send people back in time.

Ben and the T-rex

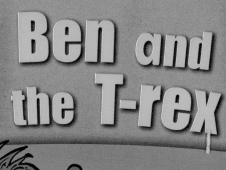

Ben ran out of the shed. "Look Ruby. I have made a time machine!" he said.

Ruby was on the swing. She stopped swinging and looked at Ben. "Your machines are rubbish!" she said.

Why does Ruby think Ben's machines are rubbish?

"This time machine could send you back in time," said Ben. "You could have your birthday all over again! It's brilliant!"

5

Ben turned the dial on the time machine. Lights flashed all over the machine.

Suddenly, a huge T-rex came out of thin air.

It opened its huge mouth and roared.

Ruby screamed and screamed.

"Whoops! I turned the dial too far," said Ben.

With a huge **CRUNCH**, the T-rex ate the swing. Then it turned to look at Ruby.

"Run, Ruby, run!" shouted Ben. Ruby screamed again and ran into the house.

But the T-rex ran into the house too.
"Oh no!" said Ben. "It could be
hungry."

The T-rex *was* hungry. With a huge
CRUNCH it ate the rubbish bin
and the kitchen light!
Then it looked at Ruby again.

What will the
T-rex eat next?

"Mum! Dad!" shouted Ben.

But Mum and Dad didn't hear.

They were listening to loud music.

The T-rex roared at Ruby.

"Ben! Do something!" screamed Ruby.
Ben turned the dial on the machine.

The lights stopped flashing.
Suddenly, the huge T-rex vanished
into thin air.

Then Mum and Dad's loud music stopped. They came into the kitchen and saw all the mess.

"Who made all this mess?" they said.

"It was a huge T-rex," said Ben.

"I made it with my time machine."

"The T-rex was hungry," said Ruby.

"It was going to eat me!"

"Nonsense!" said Dad.

"Tidy this mess or no pocket money!"
said Mum.

"This was all your fault," said Ruby.
"Yes!" said Ben. "But my next
machine will be brilliant!"

Quiz

Text Detective

- Why didn't the parents hear the dinosaur?
- Do you think Ben's next machine will be brilliant?

Word Detective

- **Phonic Focus**: Long vowels

  Page 3: Sound out the three phonemes (sounds) in 'made'. What long vowel can you hear?
- Page 7: Find a word that means 'cried loudly'.
- Page 8: Find three words ending in 'ed'.

Super Speller

Read these words:

time   next   turned

Now try to spell them!

HA! HA! HA!

Q What was T-rex's favourite number?

A 8 (ate)!

17

Find out about

- Tyrannosaurus rex – the most dangerous dinosaur

Tricky words

- dinosaur
- dangerous
- million
- heavy
- eyesight
- jaws
- balance

Introduce these tricky words and help the reader when they come across them later!

Text starter

Tyrannosaurus rex lived about 65 million years ago. It was very strong and very heavy. It had long, sharp teeth and it ate other dinosaurs.

Tyrannosaurus rex

Tyrannosaurus rex was a very big dinosaur. It was not the biggest dinosaur that ever lived, but it was the most dangerous.

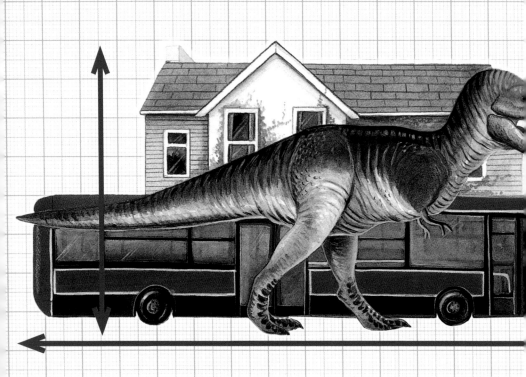

T-rex lived about 65 million years ago. It was as tall as a house and as long as a bus.

T-rex was very strong and very heavy. It was as heavy as seven elephants. That's **VERY** heavy!

T-rex was a meat-eating dinosaur.

T-rex had small arms, but very big, strong legs. Its feet were one metre long, but T-rex walked on its toes. It had three toes on each of its feet.

T-rex could step about four metres at a time. That's over four times bigger than a human step!

T-rex had a very big head and very big eyes. Each eye was four times bigger than a human eye.
It had very good eyesight!

T-rex had big, strong jaws.
It could eat other small dinosaurs
in one **CRUNCH**!

T-rex could smell very well. It could smell other dinosaurs from a long way away.

T-rex would catch the dinosaur and sink its long, sharp teeth into it. Then it would eat it.

The teeth of a T-rex have been found stuck in the bones of other dinosaurs.

T-rex had about 60 long, sharp teeth. If one of these long, sharp teeth fell out, another tooth would grow.

T-rex had a long tail. The tail helped it to balance. If T-rex did not have a long tail, it would have fallen over on to its nose!

T-rex lived in forests and near rivers.
So did the plant-eating dinosaurs.
Some of these plant-eating dinosaurs
were bigger than T-rex, but it would
catch them and eat them.

T-rex was the most dangerous dinosaur that ever lived.

Quiz

Text Detective

- Which was the most dangerous dinosaur?
- What have you learned about T-rex that you did not know before?

Word Detective

- **Phonic Focus:** Long vowels
  Page 27: Sound out the three phonemes (sounds) in 'teeth'. What long vowel can you hear?
- Page 19: How many syllables are there in 'dinosaur'?
- Page 24: Find a word made from two smaller words.

Super Speller

Read these words:

been   lived   three

Now try to spell them!

HA! HA! HA!

Q What do you call a sleeping dinosaur?

A A dinosnore!

32